FOREVER

engaged!

Real Love

love and joy

just for you

Will you be mine?

YOU MAKE ME HAPPY

I can't say I *do*
without you!

Save the Date

CELEBRATION

love you ♥

Our Story

i am
grateful

hugs +
kisses

You are my heart,
my life, my one and
only thought

I ♡ you

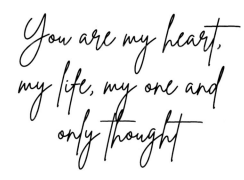

Made in the USA
Las Vegas, NV
28 November 2024

12853141R00017